Keto S  r
R

The cookbook to impress your friends at
the dinner table.
Cook healthy dishes to stop hypertension
and improve your body's health.

Odessa Renner

Furthermore, the transmission, duplication, or reproduction of any of the following work including specific information will be considered an illegal act irrespective of if it is done electronically or in print. This extends to creating a secondary or tertiary copy of the work or a recorded copy and is only allowed with the express written consent from the Publisher. All additional right reserved.

The information in the following pages is broadly considered a truthful and accurate account of facts and as such, any inattention, use, or misuse of the information in question by the reader will render any resulting actions solely under their purview. There are no scenarios in which the publisher or the original author of this work can be in any fashion deemed liable for any hardship or damages that may befall them after undertaking information described herein.

Additionally, the information in the following pages is intended only for informational purposes and should thus be thought of as universal. As befitting its nature, it is presented without assurance regarding its prolonged validity or interim quality. Trademarks that are mentioned are done without written consent and can in no way be considered an endorsement from the trademark holder.

Table of Contents

Introduction

Slow cookers can be really useful in the kitchen and can make life so much easier. They make it so that you can prep your ingredients the day before, and they will be ready for you when you get home. The slow cooker is also great for people on a tight budget, because it can save you a lot of money in the long run. That said, it's important to know how to use your slow cooker properly. Here are some tips to help you get started.

Cook With Low Heat

Always start with low heat when cooking your ingredients in a slow cooker. If you put them over medium heat, they will burn or scorch before they are finished. Instead, start out on low heat and let them cook for several hours until they are done. This will ensure that they are safe to eat and don't have any nasty flavors left over from being cooked too fast.

Leave room at the top

Place your ingredients in the cooker as soon as possible after placing them on the stove top or in the oven. This will give them enough time to cook properly without being overcooked on high heat. If you leave them sitting in the hot pot without food inside of it, sometimes it can become stuck and won't release until you turn off the burner. This can cause some parts of your dish to be overcooked, which can ruin everything you worked so hard to perfect!

Use recipes right away

A great way to use your slow cooker is by developing some new recipes! Have fun experimenting and working on some new ones all at once without having to worry about any nasty flavors ruining your dish later on. Take note of what works well and what does not, so you end up with something delicious every time!

Slow Cookers are a great way to prepare your food and make it taste like someone else has done it for you. With the right recipe in your slow cooker, you can turn days of cooking into hours of preparation.

We've decided to share with you some of our favorite slow cooker recipes from around the country. Some recipes are classic favorites, while others are new and fresh. Whatever you're looking for, you'll find it here.

Slow cookers are a great way to prepare all kinds of meals. With the right recipe, you can cook a variety of dishes, including soups that will warm you up on a cold day.

Some of the advantages to using a slow cooker include reducing the amount of energy needed to use your electric stove. You also don't have to worry about burning yourself when using the stove. You can also leave the slow cooker on when you're not home, making it easy to prepare simple meals and snacks for your family.

You can find many recipes in our slow cooker cookbook. It's divided into several sections, including breakfast, main dishes, side dishes, desserts, and drinks. The slow cooker cookbook is designed for a number of different uses. For example, you can use it to make lots of different side dishes and desserts while you're on vacation or traveling. You can also use the same cookbook in your kitchen to prepare healthy main meals during the week or when you're having friends over for dinner.

Don't let your slow cooker get rusty with age! Contact us today to order our slow cooker cookbook at our guaranteed lowest price. We'll even ship it right away so that you can get started cooking immediately!

Savoy Cabbage Mix

Preparation time: 15 minutes

Cooking time: 2 Hours

Servings: 2

Ingredients

- 1 pound Savoy cabbage, shredded
- 1 red onion, sliced
- 1 tablespoon olive oil
- ½ cup veggie stock
- A pinch of salt and black pepper
- 1 carrot, grated
- ½ cup tomatoes, cubed
- ½ teaspoon sweet paprika
- ½ inch ginger, grated

Directions:

1. In your Crock Pot, mix the cabbage with the onion, oil and the other Ingredients, toss, put the lid on and cook it on High for two hours.
2. Divide the mix between plates and serve as a side dish.

Nutrition: calories 100, fat 3, fiber 4, carbs 5, protein 2

Balsamic-glazed Beets

Preparation time: 15 minutes

Cooking time: 2 Hours

Servings: 6

Ingredients

- 1 lb. beets, sliced
- 5 oz. orange juice
- 3 oz. balsamic vinegar
- 3 tbsp. almonds
- 6 oz. goat cheese
- 1 tsp. minced garlic
- 1 tsp. olive oil

Directions:

1. Toss the beets with balsamic vinegar, orange juice, and olive oil in the insert of Crock Pot.
2. Put the slow cooker's lid on and set the cooking time to 7 hours on Low settings.
3. Toss goat cheese with minced garlic and almonds in a bowl.
4. Spread this cheese garlic mixture over the beets.
5. Put the cooker's lid on and set the cooking time to 10 minutes on High settings.

6. Serve warm.

Nutrition: Per Serving: Calories: 189, Total Fat: 11.3g, Fiber: 2g, Total Carbs: 12g, Protein: 10g

Cauliflower Rice and Spinach

Preparation time: 15 minutes

Cooking time: 3 Hours

Servings: 8

Ingredients

- 2 garlic cloves, minced
- 2 tablespoons butter, melted
- 1 yellow onion, chopped
- ¼ teaspoon thyme, dried
- 3 cups veggie stock
- 20 ounces spinach, chopped
- 6 ounces coconut cream
- Salt and black pepper to the taste
- 2 cups cauliflower rice

Directions:

1. Heat up a pan with the butter over medium heat, add onion, stir and cook for 4 minutes.
2. Add garlic, thyme and stock, stir, cook for 1 minute more and transfer to your Crock Pot.
3. Add spinach, coconut cream, cauliflower rice, salt and pepper, stir a bit, cover and cook on High for hours.
4. Divide between plates and serve as a side dish.

Nutrition: calories 200, fat 4, fibre 4, carbs 8, protein 2

Cumin Quinoa Pilaf

Preparation time: 15 minutes

Cooking time: 2 Hours

Servings: 2

Ingredients

- 1 cup quinoa
- 2 teaspoons butter, melted
- Salt and black pepper to the taste
- 1 teaspoon turmeric powder
- 2 cups chicken stock
- 1 teaspoon cumin, ground

Directions:

1. Grease your Crock Pot with the butter, add the quinoa and the other **Ingredients:**, toss, put the lid on and then cook on High for about 2 hours

2. Divide between plates and serve as a side dish.

Nutrition: calories 152, fat 3, fiber 6, carbs 8, protein 4

Balsamic Okra Mix

Preparation time: 15 minutes

Cooking time: 2 Hours

Servings: 4

Ingredients

- 2 cups okra, sliced
- 1 cup cherry tomatoes, halved
- 1 tablespoon olive oil
- ½ teaspoon turmeric powder
- ½ cup canned tomatoes, crushed
- 2 tablespoons balsamic vinegar
- 2 tablespoons basil, chopped
- 1 tablespoon thyme, chopped

Directions:

1. In your Crock Pot, mix the okra with the tomatoes, crushed tomatoes and the other Ingredients, toss, put the lid on and cook on High for 2 hours.
2. Divide between plates and serve as a side dish.

Nutrition: calories 233, fat 12, fiber 4, carbs 8, protein 4

Asparagus Mix

Preparation time: 15 minutes

Cooking time: 6 Hours

Servings: 4

Ingredients

- 10 ounces cream of celery
- 12 ounces asparagus, chopped
- 2 eggs, hard-boiled, peeled and sliced
- 1 cup cheddar cheese, shredded
- 1 teaspoon olive oil

Directions:

1. Grease your Crock Pot with the oil, add cream of celery and cheese to the Crock Pot and stir.
2. Add asparagus and eggs, cover and cook on Low for 6 hours.
3. Divide between plates and serve as a side dish.

Nutrition: calories 241, fat 5, fiber 4, carbs 5, protein 12

Tarragon Sweet Potatoes

Preparation time: 15 minutes

Cooking time: 3 Hours

Servings: 4

Ingredients

- 1 pound sweet potatoes, peeled and cut into wedges
- 1 cup veggie stock
- ½ teaspoon chili powder
- ½ teaspoon cumin, ground
- Salt and black pepper to the taste
- 1 tablespoon olive oil
- 1 tablespoon tarragon, dried
- 2 tablespoons balsamic vinegar

Directions:

1. In your Crock Pot, mix the sweet potatoes with the stock, chili powder and the other Ingredients, toss, put the lid on and cook on High for 3 hours.

2. Divide the mix between plates and serve as a side dish.

Nutrition: calories 80, fat 4, fiber 4, carbs 8, protein 4

Classic Veggies Mix

Preparation time: 15 minutes

Cooking time: 3 Hours

Servings: 4

Ingredients

- 1 and ½ cups red onion, cut into medium chunks
- 1 cup cherry tomatoes, halved
- 2 and ½ cups zucchini, sliced
- 2 cups yellow bell pepper, chopped
- 1 cup mushrooms, sliced
- 2 tablespoons basil, chopped
- 1 tablespoon thyme, chopped
- ½ cup olive oil
- ½ cup balsamic vinegar

Directions:

1. In your Crock Pot, mix onion pieces with tomatoes, zucchini, bell pepper, mushrooms, basil, thyme, oil and vinegar, toss to coat everything, cover and cook on High for 3 hours.

2. Divide between plates and serve as a side dish.

Nutrition: calories 150, fat 2, fiber 2, carbs 6, protein 5

Mint Farro Pilaf

Preparation time: 15 minutes

Cooking time: 4 Hours

Servings: 2

Ingredients

- ½ tablespoon balsamic vinegar
- ½ cup whole grain farro
- A pinch of salt and black pepper
- 1 cup chicken stock
- ½ tablespoon olive oil
- 1 tablespoon green onions, chopped
- 1 tablespoon mint, chopped

Directions:

1. In your Crock Pot, mix the farro with the vinegar and the other Ingredients, toss, put the lid on and cook on Low for 4 hours.
2. Divide between plates and serve.

Nutrition: calories 162, fat 3, fiber 6, carbs 9, protein 4

Soups and Stews

Herbed Chicken & Green Chiles Soup

Preparation time: 15 minutes

Cooking time: 6 Hours

Servings: 8 (13.1 Ounces per Serving)

Ingredients

- 2 chicken breasts, boneless, skinless

- ½ teaspoon cumin, ground

- 1 teaspoon onion powder

- 1 teaspoon chili powder

- 1 teaspoon garlic powder

- ½ teaspoon white pepper, ground

- ¼ teaspoon cayenne pepper

- 4 ounces green chilies

- 1 cup beans

- 3 cups water

- ½ avocado, cubed

- 2 tablespoons extra virgin olive oil

- 1 small carrot, diced

Directions:

1. Grease the bottom of Crock-Pot with olive oil and place chicken inside pot.

2. Mix white pepper, cumin, garlic, onion, and chili powder.

3. Sprinkle evenly over the chicken. Place the chilies on top of chicken.

4. Pour in water and add beans and carrot and stir. Close the lid and cook on HIGH for an hour.

5. Open the lid and give a good stir. Close the lid and continue to cook on HIGH for 5 hours.

6. Serve hot with avocado.

Nutrition: Calories: 180.02, Total Fat: 7.04 g, Saturated Fat: 1.19 g, Cholesterol: 18.28 mg, Sodium: 831.99 mg, Potassium: 599.6 mg, Total Carbohydrates: 9.82 g, Fiber: 3.93 g, Sugar: 1.6 g, Protein: 13.02 g

Turmeric Squash Soup

Preparation time: 15 minutes

Cooking time: 9 Hours

Servings: 6

Ingredients

- 3 chicken thighs, skinless, boneless, chopped
- 3 cups butternut squash, chopped
- 1 teaspoon ground turmeric
- 1 onion, sliced
- 1 oz. green chilies, chopped, canned
- 6 cups of water

Directions:

1. Put chicken thighs in the bottom of the Slow Cooker and top them with green chilies.

2. Then add the ground turmeric, butternut squash, and water.   Add sliced onion and close the lid.

3. Cook the soup on low for 9 Hours.

Nutrition: 194 calories, 22.6g protein, 8.4g carbohydrates, 5.8g fat, 3.2g fiber, 65mg cholesterol, 78mg sodium, 551mg potassium.

Celery Stew

Preparation time: 15 minutes

Cooking time: 6 Hours

Servings: 4

Ingredients

- 3 cups of water

- 1-pound beef stew meat, cubed

- 2 cups celery, chopped

- ½ cup cremini mushrooms, sliced

- 2 tablespoons sour cream

- 1 teaspoon smoked paprika

- 1 teaspoon cayenne pepper

- 1 tablespoon sesame oil

Directions:

1. Mix beef stew meat with cayenne pepper and put in the hot skillet.

2. Add sesame oil and roast the meat for 1 minute per side on high heat.

3. Transfer the meat in the Slow Cooker.

4. Add celery, cremini mushrooms, sour cream, smoked paprika, and water.

5. Close the lid and cook the stew on high for 6 hours.

Nutrition: 267 calories, 35.3g protein, 2.7g carbohydrates, 12g fat, 1.2g fiber, 104g cholesterol, 124mg sodium, 660mg potassium.

Barley Soup

Preparation time: 15 minutes

Cooking time: 8 Hours

Servings: 5

Ingredients

- ¼ cup barley

- 5 cups chicken stock

- 4 oz. pork tenderloin, chopped

- 1 tablespoon dried cilantro

- 1 tablespoon tomato paste

- 3 oz. carrot, grated

- ½ cup heavy cream

Directions:

1. Put pork tenderloin in the Slow Cooker.

2. Add barley, chicken stock, tomato paste, carrot, and heavy cream.

3. Carefully stir the soup mixture and close the lid.

4. Cook it on Low for 8 hours.

Nutrition: 126 calories, 8.3g protein, 10.1g carbohydrates, 6g fat, 2.2g fiber, 33mg cholesterol, 797mg sodium, 249mg potassium.

Cabbage Stew

Preparation time: 15 minutes

Cooking time: 3 Hours

Servings: 2

Ingredients

- 2 cups white cabbage, shredded

- ½ cup tomato juice

- 1 teaspoon ground white pepper

- 1 cup cauliflower, chopped

- ½ cup potato, chopped

- 1 cup of water

Directions:

1. Put cabbage, potato, and cauliflower in the Slow Cooker.

2. Add tomato juice, ground white pepper, and water. Stir the stew **Ingredients:** and close the lid.

3. Cook the stew on high for hours.

Nutrition: 57 calories, 2.8g protein, 13.3g carbohydrates, 0.2g fat, 3.9g fiber, 0mg cholesterol, 196mg sodium, 503mg potassium.

Sweet Potato & Sausage Soup

Preparation time: 15 minutes

Cooking time: 7 Hours And 35 Minutes

Servings: 6 (12.4 Ounces per Serving)

Ingredients

- 1 lb. sausage links, pork or chicken

- 8 large sweet potatoes, cubed

- 1 onion, chopped

- 1 glass red wine

- 4 tablespoons tomato sauce

Olive oil

- 3 cups water

- Salt and pepper to taste and other seasonings

- 1 cup of bacon, cooked, cubed

- 1 cup smoked ham, cooked, cubed

- 1 red pepper, diced

Directions:

1. Chop the onion into cubes. Grease a frying pan and sauté onion until golden in color, for about six minutes.

2. Add the cubed ham and bacon. Add cubed potatoes and salt and pepper to taste.

3. Pour in wine and stir. Place all **Ingredients:** in Slow Cooker.

4. Add the water and cover and cook on LOW for 6-7 hours.

5. Add the chopped pepper and tomato sauce and cook on LOW for an additional 30 minutes more.

6. Serve hot.

Nutrition: Calories: 126.71, Total Fat: 2.02 g, Saturated Fat: 0.99 g, Cholesterol: 18.33 mg, Sodium: 787.22 mg, Potassium: 215.12 mg, Total Carbohydrates: 6.95 g, Fiber: 0.52 g, Sugar: 1.26 g, Protein: 15.3 g

Coconut Cod Stew

Preparation time: 15 minutes

Cooking time: 6.5 Hours

Servings: 6

Ingredients

- 1-pound cod fillet, chopped

- 2 oz. scallions, roughly chopped

- 1 cup coconut cream

- 1 teaspoon curry powder

- 1 teaspoon garlic, diced

Directions:

1. Mix curry powder with coconut cream and garlic.

2. Add scallions and gently stir the liquid. After this, pour it in the Slow Cooker and add cod fillet.

3. Stir the stew mixture gently and close the lid.

4. Cook the stew on low for 6hours.

Nutrition: 158 calories, 14.7g protein, 3.3g carbohydrates, 10.3g fat, 1.3g fiber, 37mg cholesterol, 55mg sodium, 138mg potassium.

German Style Soup

Preparation time: 15 minutes

Cooking time: 8.5 Hours

Servings: 6

Ingredients

- 1-pound beef loin, chopped

- 6 cups of water

- 1 cup sauerkraut

- 1 onion, diced

- 1 teaspoon cayenne pepper

- ½ cup Greek yogurt

Directions:

1. Put beef and onion in the Slow Cooker.

2. Add yogurt, water, and cayenne pepper.

3. Cook the mixture on low for 8 hours.

4. When the beef is cooked, add sauerkraut and stir the soup carefully.

5. Cook the soup on high for 30 minutes.

Nutrition: 137 calories, 16.1g protein, 4.3g carbohydrates, 5.8g fat, 1.1g fiber, 41mg cholesterol, 503mg sodium, 93mg potassium.

Shrimp Chowder

Preparation time: 15 minutes

Cooking time: 1 Hour

Servings: 4

Ingredients

- 1-pound shrimps

- ½ cup fennel bulb, chopped

- 1 bay leaf

- ½ teaspoon peppercorn

- 1 cup of coconut milk

- 3 cups of water

- 1 teaspoon ground coriander

Directions:

1. Put all **Ingredients:** in the Slow Cooker.

2. Close the lid and cook the chowder on High for 1 hour.

Nutrition: 277 calories, 27.4g protein, 6.1g carbohydrates, 16.3g fat, 1.8g fiber, 239mg cholesterol, 297mg sodium, 401mg potassium.

Ground Pork Soup

Preparation time: 15 minutes

Cooking time: 5.5 Hour

Servings: 4

Ingredients

- 1 cup ground pork

- ½ cup red kidney beans, canned

- 1 cup tomatoes, canned

- 4 cups of water

- 1 tablespoon dried cilantro

- 1 teaspoon salt

Directions:

1. Put ground pork in the Slow Cooker.

2. Add tomatoes, water, dried cilantro, and salt.   Close the lid and cook the **Ingredients:** on High for 5 hours.

3. Then add canned red kidney beans and cook the soup on high for 30 minutes more.

Nutrition: 318 calories, 25.7g protein, 10.9g carbohydrates, 16.6g fat, 4.1g fiber, 74mg cholesterol, 651mg sodium, 706mg potassium.

Chinese Style Cod Stew

Preparation time: 15 minutes

Cooking time: 5 Hours

Servings: 2

Ingredients

- 6 oz. cod fillet

- 1 teaspoon sesame seeds

- 1 teaspoon olive oil

- 1 garlic clove, chopped

- ¼ cup of soy sauce

- ¼ cup fish stock

- 4 oz. fennel bulb, chopped

Directions:

1. Pour fish stock in the Slow Cooker.

2. Add soy sauce, olive oil, garlic, and sesame seeds.

3. Then chop the fish roughly and add in the Slow Cooker.

4. Cook the meal on Low for 5 hours.

Nutrition: 139 calories, 18.9g protein, 7.4g carbohydrates, 4.2g fat, 2.2g fiber, 42mg cholesterol, 1926mg sodium, 359mg potassium.

Beans Stew

Preparation time: 15 minutes

Cooking time: 5 Hours

Servings: 3

Ingredients

- ½ cup sweet pepper, chopped

- ¼ cup onion, chopped

- 1 cup edamame beans

- 1 cup tomatoes

- 1 teaspoon cayenne pepper

- 5 cups of water

- 2 tablespoons cream cheese

Directions:

1. Mix water with cream cheese and pour the liquid in the Slow Cooker.

2. Add cayenne pepper, edamame beans, and onion.

3. Then chop the tomatoes roughly and add in the Slow Cooker.

4. Close the lid and cook the stew on high for 5 hours.

Nutrition: 74 calories, 3.4g protein, 7.9g carbohydrates, 3.6g fat, 2.4g fiber, 7mg cholesterol, 109mg sodium, 218mg potassium.

Creamy Bacon Soup

Preparation time: 15 minutes

Cooking time: 1 3/4 Hours

Servings: 6

Ingredients

- 1 tablespoon olive oil

- 6 bacon slices, chopped

- 1 sweet onion, chopped

- 1 1/2 pounds potatoes, peeled and cubed

- 1 parsnip, diced

- 1/2 celery root, cubed

- 2 cups chicken stock

- 3 cups water

- Salt and pepper to taste

Directions:

1. Heat the oil in a skillet and add the bacon. Cook until crisp then remove the bacon on a plate.

2. Pour the fat of the bacon in your Slow Cooker and add the remaining Ingredients.

3. Adjust the taste with salt and pepper and cook on high settings for 1 1/2 hours.

4. When done, puree the soup with an immersion blender until smooth.

5. Pour the soup in a bowl and top with bacon.

6. Serve right away.

Nutrition: calories 187, fat 4, fiber 4, carbs 7, protein 8

Seafood Stew

Preparation time: 15 minutes

Cooking time: 7 Hours

Servings: 4

Ingredients

- 28 ounces canned tomatoes, crushed

- 4 cups veggie stock

- 3 garlic cloves, minced

- 1 pound sweet potatoes, cubed

- ½ cup yellow onion, chopped

- 2 pounds mixed seafood

- 1 teaspoon thyme, dried

- 1 teaspoon cilantro, dried

- 1 teaspoon basil, dried

- Salt and black pepper to the taste

- A pinch of red pepper flakes, crushed

Directions:

1. In your Slow Cooker, mix tomatoes with stock, garlic, sweet potatoes, onion, thyme, cilantro, basil, salt, pepper and pepper flakes, stir, cover and cook on Low for 6 hours.

2. Add seafood, stir, cover, and cook on High for 1 more hour, divide stew into bowls and serve for lunch.

Nutrition: calories 270, fat 4, fiber 4, carbs 12, protein 3

Dessert Recipes

Almond Pie

Preparation time: 15 minutes

Cooking time: 41 minutes

Servings: 8 servings

Ingredients

- 1 cup almond flour

- ½ cup of coconut milk

- 1 teaspoon vanilla extract

- 2 tablespoons butter, softened

- 1 tablespoon Truvia

- ¼ cup coconut, shredded

- 1 cup water, for cooking

Directions:

1. In the mixing bowl, mix up almond flour, coconut milk, vanilla extract, butter, Truvia, and shredded coconut.
2. When the mixture is smooth, transfer it in the baking pan and flatten.
3. Pour water and insert the steamer rack in the instant pot.
4. Put the baking pan with cake on the rack. Close and seal the lid.

5. Cook the dessert on manual mode (high pressure) for 41 minutes. Allow the natural pressure release for 10 minutes.

Nutrition: calories 90, fat 9.1, fiber 0.9, carbs 2.6, protein 1.2

Coconut Cupcakes

Preparation time: 15 minutes

Cooking time: 10 minutes

Servings: 6 servings

Ingredients

- 4 eggs, beaten

- 4 tablespoons coconut milk

- 4 tablespoons coconut flour

- ½ teaspoon vanilla extract

- 2 tablespoons Erythritol

- 1 teaspoon baking powder

- 1 cup water, for cooking

Directions:

1.   In the mixing bowl, mix up eggs, coconut milk, coconut flour, vanilla extract, Erythritol, and baking powder.

2.   Then pour the batter in the cupcake molds.

3.   Pour water and insert the steamer rack in the instant pot.

4.   Place the cupcakes on the rack. Close and seal the lid.

5.   Cook the cupcakes for 10 minutes on manual mode (high pressure).

6.   Then allow the natural pressure release for 5 minutes.

Nutrition: calories 86, fat 5.8, fiber 2.2, carbs 9.2, protein 4.6

Anise Hot Chocolate

Preparation time: 10 minutes

Cooking time: 2 minutes

Servings: 3 servings

Ingredients

- 1 tablespoon cocoa powder

- 1 tablespoon Erythritol

- ¼ cup heavy cream

- ½ cup of coconut milk

- ½ teaspoon ground anise

Directions:

1.   Put all **Ingredients** in the instant pot bowl. Stir them well until you get a smooth liquid.

2.   Close and seal the lid.

3.   Cook the hot chocolate on manual (high pressure) for 2 minutes. Then allow the natural pressure release for 5 minutes.

Nutrition: calories 131, fat 13.5, fiber 1.4, carbs 8.5, protein 1.5

Chocolate Mousse

Preparation time: 10 minutes

Cooking time: 4 minutes

Servings: 1 serving

Ingredients

- 1 egg yolk

- 1 teaspoon Erythritol

- 1 teaspoon of cocoa powder

- 2 tablespoons coconut milk

- 1 tablespoon cream cheese

- 1 cup water, for cooking

Directions:

1.   Pour water and insert the steamer rack in the instant pot.

2.   Then whisk the egg yolk with Erythritol.

3.   When the mixture turns into lemon color, add coconut milk, cream cheese, and cocoa powder. Whisk the mixture until smooth.

4.   Then pour it in the glass jar and place it on the steamer rack.

5.   Close and seal the lid.

6.   Cook the dessert on manual (high pressure) for 4 minutes. Make a quick pressure release.

Nutrition: calories 162, fat 15.4, fiber 1.2, carbs 3.5, protein 4.5

Lime Muffins

Preparation time: 10 minutes

Cooking time: 15 minutes

Servings: 6 servings

Ingredients

- 1 teaspoon lime zest

- 1 tablespoon lemon juice

- 1 teaspoon baking powder

- 1 cup almond flour

- 2 eggs, beaten

- 1 tablespoon swerve

- ¼ cup heavy cream

- 1 cup water, for cooking

Directions:

1. In the mixing bowl, mix up lemon juice, baking powder, almond flour, eggs, swerve, and heavy cream.

2. When the muffin batter is smooth, add lime zest and mix it up.

3. Fill the muffin molds with batter.

4. Then pour water and insert the rack in the instant pot.

5. Place the muffins on the rack. Close and seal the lid.

6. Cook the muffins on manual (high pressure) for 15 minutes.

7. Then allow the natural pressure release.

Nutrition: calories 153, fat 12.2, fiber 2.1, carbs 5.1, protein 6

Blueberry Muffins

Preparation time: 15 minutes

Cooking time: 14 minutes

Servings: 3 servings

Ingredients

¼ cup blueberries

¼ teaspoon baking powder

1 teaspoon apple cider vinegar

4 teaspoons butter, melted

2 eggs, beaten

1 cup coconut flour

2 tablespoons Erythritol

1 cup water, for cooking

Directions:

1.   In the mixing bowl, mix up baking powder, apple cider vinegar, butter, eggs, coconut flour, and Erythritol.

2.   When the batter is smooth, add blueberries. Stir well.

3.   Put the muffin batter in the muffin molds.

4.   After this, pour water and insert the steamer rack in the instant pot.

5.   Then place the muffins on the rack. Close and seal the lid.

6.   Cook the muffins on manual mode (high pressure) for 14 minutes.

7.   When the time is finished, allow the natural pressure release for 6 minutes.

Nutrition: calories 95, fat 4.5, fiber 6.1, carbs 14.6, protein 3.4

Low Carb Brownie

Preparation time: 15 minutes

Cooking time: 15 minutes

Servings: 8 servings

Ingredients

- 1 cup coconut flour

- 1 tablespoon cocoa powder

- 1 tablespoon coconut oil

- 1 teaspoon vanilla extract

- 1 teaspoon baking powder

- 1 teaspoon apple cider vinegar

- 1/3 cup butter, melted

- 1 tablespoon Erythritol

- 1 cup water, for cooking

Directions:

1.   In the mixing bowl, mix up Erythritol, melted butter, apple cider vinegar, baking powder, vanilla extract, coconut oil, cocoa powder, and coconut flour.

2.   Whisk the mixture until smooth and pour it in the baking pan. Flatten the surface of the batter.

3.   Pour water and insert the steamer rack in the instant pot.

4.   Put the pan with brownie batter on the rack. Close and seal the lid.

5.   Cook the brownie on manual mode (high pressure) for 15 minutes.

6.   Then allow the natural pressure release for 5 minutes.

7.   Cut the cooked brownies into the bars.

Nutrition: calories 146, fat 11, fiber 6.2, carbs 12.6, protein 2.2

Pecan Pie

Preparation time: 20 minutes

Cooking time: 25 minutes

Servings: 4 servings

Ingredients

- 2 tablespoons coconut oil

- 4 tablespoons almond flour

- 4 pecans, chopped

- 1 tablespoon Erythritol

- 2 tablespoons butter

- 1 tablespoon coconut flour

- 1 cup water, for cooking

Directions:

1. Make the pie crust: mix up coconut oil and almond flour in the bowl.

2. Then knead the dough and put it in the baking pan. Flatten the dough in the shape of the pie crust.

3. Then melt Erythritol, butter, and coconut flour.

4. When the mixture is liquid, add chopped pecans.

5. Pour water in the instant pot and insert the steamer rack.

6. Pour the butter-pecan mixture over the pie crust, flatten it and transfer on the steamer rack.

7. Cook the pecan pie on manual mode (high pressure) for 25 minutes.

8. Allow the natural pressure release for 10 minutes and cool the cooked pie well.

Nutrition: calories 257, fat 26.1, fiber 3, carbs 8.5, protein 3.3

Vanilla Flan

Preparation time: 10 minutes

Cooking time: 8 minutes

Servings: 4 servings

Ingredients

- 4 egg whites

- 4 egg yolks

- ½ cup Erythritol

- 7 oz. heavy cream, whipped

- 3 tablespoons water

- 1 tablespoon butter

- ½ teaspoon vanilla extract

- 1 cup water, for cooking

Directions:

1.   In the saucepan, heat up Erythritol and butter. When the mixture is smooth, leave it in a warm place.

2.   Meanwhile, mix up water, heavy cream, egg whites, and egg yolks. Whisk the mixture.

3.   Pour the Erythritol mixture in the flan ramekins and then add heavy cream mixture over the sweet mixture.

4.   Pour water and insert the steamer rack in the instant pot.

5.   Place the ramekins with flan on the rack. Close and seal the lid.

6.   Cook the dessert on manual (high pressure) for 10 minutes. Then allow the natural pressure release for 10 minutes.

7.   Cool the cooked flan for 25 minutes.

Nutrition: calories 269, fat 25.8, fiber 0, carbs 2.3, protein 7.4

Vanilla Pie

Preparation time: 20 minutes

Cooking time: 35 minutes

Servings: 12 servings

Ingredients

- 1 cup heavy cream

- 3 eggs, beaten

- 1 teaspoon vanilla extract

- ¼ cup Erythritol

- 1 cup coconut flour

- 1 tablespoon butter, melted

- 1 cup water, for cooking

Directions:

1.   In the mixing bowl, mix up coconut flour, Erythritol, vanilla extract, eggs, and heavy cream.

2.   Grease the baking pan with melted butter.

3.   Pour the coconut mixture in the baking pan.

4.   Pour water and insert the steamer rack in the instant pot.

5.   Place the pie on the rack. Close and seal the lid.

6.   Cook the pie on manual mode (high pressure) for 35 minutes.

7.   Allow the natural pressure release for 10 minutes.

Nutrition: calories 100, fat 6.8, fiber 4, carbs 12.1, protein 2.9

Custard

Preparation time: 10 minutes

Cooking time: 7 minutes

Servings: 4 servings

Ingredients

6 eggs, beaten

1 cup heavy cream

1 teaspoon vanilla extract

¼ teaspoon ground nutmeg

2 tablespoons Erythritol

1 tablespoon coconut flour

1 cup water, for cooking

Directions:

1. Whisk the eggs and Erythritol until smooth.

2. Then add heavy cream, vanilla extract, ground nutmeg, and coconut flour.

3. Whisk the mixture well again.

4. Then pour it in the custard ramekins and cover with foil.

5. Pour water and insert the steamer rack in the instant pot.

6. Place the ramekins with custard on the rack. Close and seal the lid.

7. Cook the meal on manual (high pressure) for 7 minutes. Make a quick pressure release.

Nutrition: calories 209, fat 17.9, fiber 0.8, carbs 10.3, protein 9.2

Crème Brule

Preparation time: 25 minutes

Cooking time: 10 minutes

Servings: 2 servings

Ingredients

1 cup heavy cream

5 egg yolks

2 tablespoons swerve

1 cup water, for cooking

Directions:

1.   Whisk the egg yolks and swerve together.

2.   Then add heavy cream and stir the mixture carefully.

3.   Pour the mixture in ramekins and place them on the steamer rack.

4.   Pour water in the instant pot. Add steamer rack with ramekins.

5.   Close and seal the lid.

6.   Cook crème Brule for 10 minutes – High pressure. Allow the natural pressure release for 15 minutes.

Nutrition: calories 347, fat 33.5, fiber 0, carbs 5.2, protein 8

Lava Cake

Preparation time: 15 minutes

Cooking time: 18 minutes

Servings: 4 servings

Ingredients

1 teaspoon baking powder

1 tablespoon cocoa powder

1 cup coconut cream

1/3 cup coconut flour

1 tablespoon almond flour

2 teaspoons Erythritol

1 tablespoon butter, melted

1 cup water, for cooking

Directions:

1. Whisk together baking powder, cocoa powder, coconut cream, coconut flour, almond flour, Erythritol, and butter.

2. Then pour the chocolate mixture in the baking cups.

3. Pour water in the instant pot. Insert the steamer rack.

4. Place the cups with cake mixture on the rack. Close and seal the lid.

5.   Cook the lava cakes on manual (high pressure) for 4 minutes. Allow the natural pressure release for 5 minutes.

Nutrition: calories 218, fat 19.2, fiber 5.9, carbs 14.2, protein 3.4

Lemon Cake

Preparation time: 15 minutes

Cooking time: 3 hours

Servings: 8

Ingredients:

1 ½ cup ground almonds

½ cup coconut flakes

6 Tablespoons sweetener like Swerve (Erythritol, or a suitable substitute)

2 teaspoons baking powder

Pinch of salt

½ cup softened coconut oil

½ cup cooking cream

2 Tablespoons lemon juice

Zest from two lemons

2 eggs

Topping:

3 tablespoons Swerve (or a suitable substitute)

½ cup boiling water

2 Tablespoons lemon juice

2 Tablespoons softened coconut oil

Directions:

In a bowl, combine the almonds, coconut, sweetener, baking powder. Whisk until combined.

In a separate bowl, blend coconut oil, cream, juice, and eggs.

Add the egg mixture to the dry fixing, mix.

Line the slow cooker with aluminum foil, pour in the batter.

In a bowl, mix the topping. Pour it over the cake batter.

Cover it with paper towels to absorb the water.

Cover, cook on high for 3 hours. Serve warm.

Nutrition:

Calories: 142

Carbs: 0g

Fat: 8g

Protein: 0g

Raspberry & Coconut Cake

Preparation time: 15 minutes

Cooking time: 3 hours

Servings: 10

Ingredients:

2 cups ground almonds

1 cup shredded coconut

¾ cup sweetener, Swerve (or a suitable substitute)

2 teaspoon baking soda

¼ teaspoon salt

4 large eggs

½ cup melted coconut oil

¾ cup of coconut milk

1 cup raspberries, fresh or frozen

½ cup sugarless dark chocolate chips

Directions:

Butter the slow cooker.

In a bowl, mix the dry ingredients.

Beat in the eggs, melted coconut oil, and coconut milk. Mix in the raspberries plus chocolate chips.

Combine the cocoa, almonds, and salt in a bowl.

Pour the batter into the buttered slow cooker.

Cover the slow cooker with a paper towel to absorb the water.

Cover, cook on low for 3 hours. Let the cake cool in the pot.

Nutrition:

Calories: 201

Carbs: 24g

Fat: 10g

Protein: 0g

Chocolate Cheesecake

Preparation time: 15 minutes

Cooking time: 2.5 hours

Servings: 8

Ingredients:

3 cups cream cheese

Pinch of salt

3 eggs

1 cup powder sweetener of your choice, Swerve (or a suitable substitute)

1 teaspoon vanilla extract

½ cup sugarless dark chocolate chips

Directions:

Whisk the cream cheese, sweetener, and salt in a bowl.

Add the eggs one at a time. Combine thoroughly.

Spread the cheesecake in a cake pan, which fits in the slow cooker you are using.

Dissolved the chocolate chips in a small pot and pour over the batter. Using a knife, swirl the chocolate through the batter.

Put 2 cups of water inside the slow cooker and set the cake pan inside. Cover it with a paper towel to absorb the water, then cook on high for 2.5 hours. Remove from the slow cooker and let it cool in the pan for 1 hour. Refrigerate.

Nutrition:

Calories: 330

Carbs: 34g

Fat: 19g

Protein: 6g

Peanut Butter & Chocolate Cake

Preparation time: 15 minutes

Cooking time: 4 hours

Servings: 12

Ingredients:

1 Tablespoon butter for greasing the slow cooker

2 cups almond flour

¾ cup sweetener of your choice

¼ cup coconut flakes

¼ cup whey protein powder

1 teaspoon baking powder

¼ teaspoon salt

¾ cup peanut butter, melted

4 large eggs

1 teaspoon vanilla extract

½ cup of water

3 Tablespoons sugarless dark chocolate, melted

Directions:

Grease the slow cooker well.

In a bowl, mix the dry ingredients. Stir in the wet ingredients one at a time.

Spread about 2/3 of batter in the slow cooker, add half the chocolate. Swirl with a fork. Top up with the remaining batter and chocolate. Swirl again.

—

Cook on low for 4 hours. Switch off. Let it sit covered for 30 minutes.

Nutrition:

Calories: 270

Carbs: 39g

Fat: 11g

Protein: 5g

Berry & Coconut Cake

Preparation time: 15 minutes

Cooking time: 2 hours

Servings: 8

Ingredients:

1 Tablespoon butter for greasing the crock

1 cup almond flour

¾ cup sweetener of your choice

1 teaspoon baking soda

¼ teaspoon salt

1 large egg, beaten with a fork

¼ cup coconut flour

¼ cup of coconut milk

2 Tablespoons coconut oil

4 cups fresh or frozen blueberries and raspberries

Directions:

Butter the slow cooker well.

In a bowl, whisk the egg, coconut milk, and oil together.

Mix the dry ingredients. Slowly stir in the wet ingredients. Do not over mix.

Pour the batter in the slow cooker, spread evenly. Spread the berries on top.

Cover, cook on high for 2 hours. Cool in the crock for 1-2 hours.

Nutrition:

Calories: 263

Carbs: 9g

Fat: 22g

Protein: 5g

Cocoa Pudding Cake

Preparation time: 15 minutes

Cooking time: 3 hours

Servings: 10

Ingredients:

1 Tablespoon butter for greasing the slow cooker

1 ½ cups ground almonds

¾ cup sweetener, Swerve (or a suitable substitute)

¾ cup cocoa powder

¼ cup whey protein

2 teaspoons baking powder

¼ teaspoon salt

4 large eggs

½ cup butter, melted

¾ cup full-fat cream

1 teaspoon vanilla extract

Directions:

Butter the slow cooker thoroughly.

Whisk the dry fixing in a bowl.

Stir in the melted butter, eggs, cream, and vanilla.

Mix well.

Pour the batter into the slow cooker and spread evenly.

Cook within 2½ to 3 hours, low. If preferred – more like pudding, cook cake shorter; more dry cake, cook longer.

Cool in the slow cooker for 30 minutes. Cut and serve.

Nutrition:

Calories: 250

Carbs: 29g

Fat: 5g

Protein: 22g

Keto Coconut Hot Chocolate

Preparation time: 15 minutes

Cooking time: 4 hours

Servings: 8

Ingredients

- 5 cups full-fat coconut milk
- 2 cups heavy cream
- 1 tsp vanilla extract
- 1/3 cup cocoa powder
- 3 ounces dark chocolate, roughly chopped
- ½ tsp cinnamon
- Few drops of stevia to taste

Directions:

1. Add the coconut milk, cream, vanilla extract, cocoa powder, chocolate, cinnamon, and stevia to the slow cooker and stir to combine.

2. Cook for 4 hours, high, whisking every 45 minutes.

3. Taste the hot chocolate and if you prefer more sweetness, add a few more drops of stevia.

Nutrition:

Calories: 135

Carbs: 5g

Fat: 11g

Protein: 5g

Ambrosia

Preparation time: 15 minutes

Cooking time: 3 hours

Servings: 10

Ingredients

- 1 cup unsweetened shredded coconut
- ¾ cup slivered almonds
- 3 ounces dark chocolate (high cocoa percentage), roughly chopped
- 1/3 cup pumpkin seeds
- 2 ounces salted butter
- 1 tsp cinnamon
- 2 cups heavy cream
- 2 cups full-fat Greek yogurt
- 1 cup fresh berries – strawberries and raspberries are best

Directions:

1. Place the shredded coconut, slivered almonds, dark chocolate, pumpkin seeds, butter, and cinnamon into the slow cooker.
2. Cook for 3 hours, high, stirring every 45 minutes to combine the chocolate and butter as it melts.
3. Remove the mixture from the slow cooker, place in a bowl, and leave to cool.

4. In a large bowl, whip the cream until softly whipped.
5. Stir the yogurt through the cream.
6. Slice the strawberries into pieces, then put it to the cream mixture, along with the other berries you are using, fold through.
7. Sprinkle the cooled coconut mixture over the cream mixture.

Nutrition:

Calories: 57

Carbs: 11g

Fat: 1g

Protein: 1g

Dark Chocolate and Peppermint Pots

Preparation time: 15 minutes

Cooking time: 2 hours

Servings: 6

Ingredients

- 2 ½ cups heavy cream
- 3 ounces dark chocolate, melted in the microwave

- 4 egg yolks, lightly beaten with a fork
- Few drops of stevia
- Few drops of peppermint essence to taste

Directions:

1. Mix the beaten egg yolks, cream, stevia, melted chocolate, and peppermint essence in a medium-sized bowl.
2. Prepare the pots by greasing 6 ramekins with butter.
3. Pour the chocolate mixture into the pots evenly.
4. Put the pots inside the slow cooker and put hot water below halfway up.
5. Cook for 2 hours, high. Take the pots out of the slow cooker and leave to cool and set.
6. Serve with a fresh mint leaf and whipped cream.

Nutrition:

Calories: 125

Carbs: 15g

Fat: 6g

Protein: 1g

Creamy Vanilla Custard

Preparation time: 15 minutes

Cooking time: 3 hours

Servings: 8

Ingredients

- 3 cups full-fat cream
- 4 egg yolks, lightly beaten
- 2 tsp vanilla extract
- Few drops of stevia

Directions:

1. Mix the cream, egg yolks, vanilla extract, and stevia in a medium-sized bowl.
2. Pour the mixture into a heat-proof dish. Place the dish into the slow cooker.
3. Put hot water into the pot, around the dish, halfway up. Set the temperature to high.
4. Cook for 3 hours. Serve hot or cold!

Nutrition:

Calories: 206

Carbs: 30g

Fat: 7g

Protein: 6g

Coconut, Chocolate, and Almond Truffle Bake

Preparation time: 15 minutes

Cooking time: 4 hours

Servings: 8

Ingredients

- 3 ounces butter, melted
- 3 ounces dark chocolate, melted
- 1 cup ground almonds
- 1 cup desiccated coconut

- 3 tbsp. unsweetened cocoa powder
- 2 tsp vanilla extract
- 1 cup heavy cream
- A few extra squares of dark chocolate, grated
- ¼ cup toasted almonds, chopped

Directions:

1. In a large bowl, mix the melted butter, chocolate, ground almonds, coconut, cocoa powder, and vanilla extract.
2. Roll the mixture into balls. Grease a heat-proof dish.
3. Place the balls into the dish—Cook for 4 hours, low setting.
4. Leave the truffle dish to cool until warm. Mix the cream until soft peak.
5. Spread the cream over the truffle dish and sprinkle the grated chocolate and chopped toasted almonds over the top. Serve immediately!

Nutrition:

Calories: 115

Carbs: 8g

Fat: 10g

Protein: 2g

Peanut Butter, Chocolate, and Pecan Cupcakes

Preparation time: 15 minutes

Cooking time: 4 hours

Servings: 14

Ingredients

- 14 paper cupcake cases
- 1 cup smooth peanut butter
- 2 ounces butter
- 2 tsp vanilla extract
- 5 ounces dark chocolate
- 2 tbsp. coconut oil
- 2 eggs, lightly beaten
- 1 cup ground almonds
- 1 tsp baking powder
- 1 tsp cinnamon
- 10 pecan nuts, toasted and finely chopped

Directions:

1. Dissolve the dark chocolate plus coconut oil in the microwave, stir to combine, and set aside.

2. Place the peanut butter and butter into a medium-sized bowl, microwave for 30 seconds at a time until the butter has just melted.

3. Mix the peanut butter plus butter until combined and smooth.

4. Stir the vanilla extract into the peanut butter mixture.

5. Mix the ground almonds, eggs, baking powder, and cinnamon in a small bowl.

6. Pour the melted chocolate and coconut oil evenly into the 14 paper cases.

7. Spoon half of the almond/egg mixture evenly into the cases, on top of the chocolate and press down slightly.

8. Spoon the peanut butter mixture into the cases, on top of the almond/egg mixture.

9. Spoon the remaining almond/egg mixture into the cases.

10. Put the pecans on top of each cupcake.

11. Put the filled cases into the slow cooker— Cook for 4 hours, high setting.

Nutrition:

Calories: 145

Carbs: 20g

Fat: 3g

Protein: 4g

Vanilla and Strawberry Cheesecake

Preparation time: 15 minutes

Cooking time: 6 hours

Servings: 8

Ingredients

- Base:
- 2 ounces butter, melted
- 1 cup ground hazelnuts
- ½ cup desiccated coconut
- 2 tsp vanilla extract
- 1 tsp cinnamon
- Filling:
- 2 cups cream cheese
- 2 eggs, lightly beaten
- 1 cup sour cream
- 2 tsp vanilla extract
- 8 large strawberries, chopped

Directions:

1. Mix the melted butter, hazelnuts, coconut, vanilla, and cinnamon in a medium-sized bowl.
2. Press the base into a greased heat-proof dish.
3. Mix the cream cheese, eggs, sour cream, and vanilla extract, beat with electric egg beaters in a large bowl until thick and combined.

4. Fold the strawberries through the cream cheese mixture.
5. Put the cream cheese batter into the dish, on top of the base, spread out until smooth.
6. Put it in the slow cooker and put hot water around the dish until halfway up.
7. Cook for 6 hours, low setting until just set but slightly wobbly.
8. Chill before serving.

Nutrition:

Calories: 156

Carbs: 4g

Fat: 7g

Protein: 15g